ANN HECHT

textiles from
guatemala

THE BRITISH MUSEUM PRESS

There's a place in the fields which is so wonderful and pretty and shady that all the girls get together – seven or eight of us – and sit under the trees and hang up our weaving. We talk and weave. It is how we enjoy ourselves with our friends. RIGOBERTA `MENCHU. 1984

I would like to think of this book as a celebration of the creative powers of the weavers whose textiles we have chosen to illustrate on these pages. The weavers come from villages and towns in the southwest highlands. For those not familiar with the geography of Guatemala, the running headlines of the design portfolio section give the department name followed by the place name (which in some cases are the same). A H

First published in 2001 by The British Museum Press
A division of The British Museum Company Ltd
46 Bloomsbury Street, London WC1B 3QQ

A catalogue record for this book is available from the British Library

ISBN 0-7141-2739-6

Commissioning Editor: Suzannah Gough
Designer: Paul Welti
Cartographer: Olive Pearson
Origination in Singapore by Imago
Printing and binding in Singapore by Imago

COVER: Fringed cloth from El Quiché , Nebaj.
INSIDE COVER: Detail from a girl's belt from Nahualá.
PREVIOUS PAGES: Brocading from a young girl's huipil. Nahualá.
THESE PAGES: Details of the brocading on the cuffs of a boy's shirt. Nahualá.

contents

Opposite are details from a selection of textiles

TOP: Small embroidered panel worked in chain stitch on a girl's *huipil*. San Juan La Laguna.

LEFT: Embroidered *randa* covering a *huipil* seam. Quezaltenango. (See pages 26-7)

RIGHT: Glimpse of a large ceremonial *huipil*. San Pedro Sacatepéqez, Department of Guatemala. (See pages 76-7)

BELOW: Tapestry woven parrot, part of the central motif of a women's headdress. San Antonio Aguas Calientes. (See pages 66-7)

introduction

Guatemala is the northernmost republic of Central America. It lies between the Caribbean Sea and the Pacific Ocean, bordered by Mexico in the north and north-west, Belize in the east, and Honduras and San Salvador in the south-east. A beautiful country, geographically diverse, it embraces snow-clad mountains and volcanoes, rain-drenched jungles, fertile coastal plains and dense rainforests, not to mention one of the most beautiful lakes in the world, Lake Atitlán.

It is the textiles of the Maya Indians in the south-west highlands, and the examples of their unique woven costume in the British

The winding road up to Todos Santos Cuchamatán, one of the more remote villages where the men still wear distinctive costume.

Museum collection, that are the subjects of this book.

The apogee of classic Maya civilization occurred between the third and ninth centuries A.D. Centuries later, in the early sixteenth century, their descendants were conquered by the Spanish, and from that time to the present day the Maya Indians have been asserting their right to maintain their own way of life. Today several million Maya still speak a host of different dialects and preserve a distinctive culture and lifestyle. The women weave and wear their own costume (each town and village has its own style), as did their mothers and grandmothers before them, to assert an ethnic identity that is rooted in history. The rhythm of life has changed little in the remoter villages, each day starting with the mother grinding corn for making tortillas on the flat rectangular stone called a *metate*.

WOMEN'S COSTUME

It may be an exaggeration to say that every Maya woman weaves, because there are always exceptions, but it is the norm; weaving is part of a woman's domestic role, together with cooking, cleaning, care of the children and helping in the fields with crops and livestock. The time spent weaving may be the most sociable part of the day for Maya women. Their portable looms (of which more later) can be set up wherever there is a suitable post or tree on which to attach them in a place where a group of friends or extended family can come together and weave companionably.

First and foremost they weave the family's clothes. The most important item of a woman's costume (*traje*) — on which she lavishes her attention — is the *huipil*, which can loosely be described as a blouse. It is this garment in particular that identifies the Maya Indian as belonging to a particular village. The basic shape of a *huipil* is rectangular and it is made up of one, two or three panels sewn together. The side seams are either left free or sewn up the side as far as the armhole. The length of the *huipil* varies; it may be short and worn loose outside the skirt, or long with the undecorated part tucked inside. A question that is often asked is 'how long does it take to weave a *huipil*?', but this is rather like asking 'how long is a piece of string?'. Ultimately it depends on how elaborate the design is, and how much time is at the weaver's disposal

An elderly couple awaiting a procession in Santiago Atitlán. The 8-metre long hair ribbon seen here is now seldom worn.

Women from Todos Santos. The style of their *huipils* is distinctive, although each individual one is different.

each day. Certainly a carefully woven, complicated design could take one or two months to complete.

Women may also weave the other parts of their costume — the skirt, *tzute* (an all-purpose carrying cloth), hair ribbon and belt — but these items, except for the *tzute*, have tended to become the work of specialist weavers using different types of loom, and in some cases the weaving of them is connected with a particular town. For example, the skirt that each woman used to weave for herself can now be bought, cut to the correct length, from the market. There are two basic types of skirt: the more common, made from a piece of material about 3 m (9 ft 10 in) in length, is worn wrapped around the waist or made up into a tube to step into; the other type, worn in Quezaltenango and Cobán, consists of as much as 6–9 m (20–30 ft) of material gathered up by a drawstring. These skirts are woven on a European-type treadle loom by men who either, like the women, fit their weaving in with the other commitments of their daily life, or alternatively have been trained in the craft of weaving and work at it full-time.

An important element in the production of fabrics is the dyeing, especially since the skirt material now popular is the type decorated with ikat designs (known in Guatemala as *jaspe*), which needs specific preparation before the thread can be dyed (see pp. 30–31). In Salcajá one sees the long warps stretched out in the road, with members of the dyer's family, even quite small children, diligently binding those areas of the design that are to remain white after the dyeing process.

The components of the women's costumes do not change with the seasons. A festival or wedding might be an occasion for a new outfit, but otherwise clothes are discarded only when no further wear can be got from them. Sometimes the life of the precious brocaded area of a garment is extended by cutting it out and incorporating it into new material.

MEN'S COSTUME AND OTHER TEXTILES

For both political and practical reasons, most Mayan men no longer wear *traje* in their daily lives. However, tourists may still see them in traditional costume in Sololá and some of the

Market day in Todos Santos. Here the men crochet their own bags, which are also eagerly bought by tourists.

villages around Lake Atitlán, and travellers venturing further afield — into the Cuchumatánes mountains, for example — will be astounded, on reaching Todos Santos, to see all the males, from the smallest boy to the oldest man, wearing red trousers striped with white, and white shirts striped with red.

Also, the shoulder bag (which in Todos Santos the men crochet themselves) remains an important accessory even in towns and villages where the men have otherwise abandoned traditional dress.

In these places there are occasions, too, when traditional clothing is worn by members of *cofradías*, religious brotherhoods attached to the church. People visiting the Sunday market in Chichicastenango are sure to catch a glimpse of the unusual trousers and jacket worn by members of the *cofradía* for processions and local customs (*costumbres*) connected with the Church of Santo Tomás (see p. 35). Women connected with the church or married to a *cofradía* member may also wear special clothing on such occasions. For example, in Quezaltenango they wear a voluminous, decorated white muslin garment made up in the shape of a *huipil* but worn like a veil, with the neck opening used to frame the face, and in Tecpán a larger *sobrehuipil* is worn over the everyday one.

In addition to the weaving of textiles for personal use and for local consumption, there is now a growing trade in crafts made for the tourist trade and export. Traditional items of costume made for the family are also to be found on sale on the street and in the markets, but in general they are of interest only to the collector; passing travellers are more likely to want to buy as a memento something that will be of use once they get home. For this reason, a new class of goods (not represented in the Museum's collection) has joined the weaver's repertoire: sets of table linen, cushion covers, men's shirts and jackets, special babies' hats, purses, or — for those who want something more 'ethnic' — small hangings, still on the looms on which they were woven. To market this new range, co-operatives have been set up to enable the weavers to manage their own purchase of materials and sale of goods, allowing them to maintain high standards without interference from, or loss of profit to, a middleman. The sale of these goods brings in welcome additional income, especially to the women who traditionally work at home.

MATERIALS

The most widely used fibre in Guatemalan textiles is cotton. The two types indigenous to Central America are a long staple white cotton

(*Gossypium hirsutum*) and a short staple brown cotton (*G. Mexicanum*). Cotton is grown in Guatemala's Pacific Lowlands, but not in sufficient quantities to meet the country's

A ball of hand-spun brown cotton.

needs. Additional raw cotton is therefore imported from Nicaragua and the USA (much of it for spinning in the Cantel factory in the district of Quezaltenango); ready-spun and dyed cotton is also imported. Highland labour is used for harvesting the cotton, which involves a yearly migration to the south by some or all of the family, looked on by the Maya Indian as an unpleasant necessity to augment the household income.

The production of wool was not known in ancient times: sheep were a post-Conquest introduction, mainly in the mountainous regions of the south-west. The largest market and centre for wool preparation and weaving is Momostenango, well known for its woollen blankets. The concentration of wool production in this area can be accounted for by its lack of good arable land for crops, coupled with the incidence of hot springs, ideal for the finishing processes and felting of woollen goods. Lengths of woollen suiting are also woven here, as well as in other centres such as Chichicastenango, Nahualá and Sololá.

Maguey fibre, extracted from the agave plant, is used in the making of nets, bags and parts of the back-strap loom. A centre for its preparation is San Pablo La Laguna and neighbouring villages on the western shores of Lake Atitlán. Here the leaves are cut from the plants, beaten, soaked and the fleshy parts scraped; finally, they are rinsed until only the maguey fibres remain. These are then spun and plied into twines, cords and ropes of various thickness.

Silkworms are not cultivated in Guatemala, so all silk used in brocading or embroidery has to be imported. This makes it expensive, but as it is sold in small quantities it can be bought a little at a time. Silk is used in special garments or items for church use, and is especially popular for working the *randas* that cover joins. The particular qualities of silk that make it so desirable are its lustre and its affinity for dyes. The silk sold is of two kinds: silk floss, an unspun silk admirably suited to brocading; and a reeled two-ply silk thread used by ribbon weavers. Rayon, an artificial silk made from reconstituted cellulose, is also lustrous — and considerably cheaper.

Acrylic is an entirely man-made fibre that can be spun to resemble a 'lofty' wool. Traditionally, most decorative brocading was worked in wool, stranded cotton or silk, but recently, due to its low cost, acrylic has begun to take their place. One consequence of this is a change in traditional colour schemes, since the acrylics seem to lend themselves to much brighter, or (dare one say?) synthetic, colours.

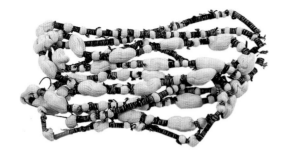

Jaspe thread, tied up ready for dyeing. Once it has been dyed, the ties are removed, revealing the design.

DYES

Although the natural dyes that were employed before the invention of chemical ones in 1856 are no longer in use (with the possible exception of indigo), some are of such historical interest that I have included the most important of them here. Such a one was the purple dye *purpura*, extracted from the saliva of molluscs found on the coast. Two molluscs would be rubbed against each other and fine strands of cotton or silk dipped into the excretion thus produced, which dyed them the prized mauve colour. The molluscs were then thrown back into the sea, having come to no apparent harm.

Cochineal is an equally intriguing dye, although its importance for Guatemala was more in connection with its export (the largest in the world prior to 1856) than its use in textiles. This is because the bright red colouring matter contained in the dried body of the female cochineal beetle (*Dactylopius coccus*) is ideal for dyeing wool and silk, but, as we have already seen, the main fibre used in Guatemalan textiles is cotton. Cochineal can, though, be found in textiles of the late nineteenth century, when wool or silk was used for brocading or in embroidery. A red dye that proved exceedingly popular for cotton was alizarin, a synthetic dye patented in 1871. It was around this time that several items of *traje* changed to red, where previously they had been white or indigo. The demise of alizarin came when the deteriorating political climate in Europe forced up its price and many cheaper dyes came on to the market.

The most widely used dye is indigo, which was another important export product, its success reaching a peak during the eighteenth century. Indigo is a dye which crosses the divide between natural and man-made because the synthetic version has the same molecular structure as the plant material and is treated in the same way. All the medium to dark blue textiles in the British Museum collection are indigo-dyed: the earlier plain skirts, before *jaspe* became the popular choice, and beautiful *perrajes* (shawls) with *jaspe* stripes, ending in intricate fringes or large pompoms, as worn in Quezaltenango. It seems, though, that now even the synthetic variety of indigo is considered too expensive and dyers are turning to other colours and more easily applied dyes as an alternative.

LOOMS

Traditionally, the back-strap loom (also known as the hip loom, body-tensioned loom or stick loom) is the one used by women. It has survived unchanged at least since the late

Stall selling looms in the market at Chichicastenango. The loom is no more than an assemblage of rods.

classic period (AD 600–800), as can be seen from depictions of it in little pottery figurines of that period. The various names for this loom add up to a simple description of how it looks and how it is used. For example, the loom without any work on it is nothing more than a bundle of sticks (hence 'stick loom') or, to be more precise, rods, which are all you will find on a stall selling looms in the market. When the loom is 'dressed', i.e. ready for weaving with all the warp threads spread out between the front and back rods, it has to be stretched out so that the threads are under tension. Both ends of the front rod are attached to a strap which circles the weaver's hips. The back rod is attached by a cord to a fixed point such as a hook, or tied by a rope to a post or tree. When the weaver sits at her loom the warp threads are held taut, or can be relaxed, according to the movement of her

A woman weaving on the back-strap loom. This is a longer warp than usual; such a warp would be necessary, for example, for trouser legs.

body (i.e. the loom is 'body-tensioned'). Before she can commence weaving she inserts another two rods (see shed rod and heddle rod in glossary) to separate alternate warp threads. The loom is now ready for weaving (that is, inserting the weft); at the end of each day the work is unhooked and it is rolled up and stowed away.

The back-strap loom is best suited to weaving comparatively small rectangles of cloth. For weaving bolts of cloth or large textiles such as blankets, the European four-shaft treadle loom, introduced by the

Spaniards, is used. This is a large wooden structure in which the lifting and lowering of the warp threads is controlled by the feet (by means of cords attached to the shafts holding the heddles), considerably reducing the time taken to weave. The warp beam can hold extremely long warps, as much as 65 m (213 ft), and the four shafts allow for the weaving of a greater number of basic structures.

A few more looms play their part in Guatemalan weaving. A small ribbon loom, perhaps unique to Guatemala, combines the body-tensioning principles of the back-strap loom with the heddle lifting mechanism of the treadle loom: a true hybrid! Two other, more sophisticated looms are in use, mainly (although not exclusively) around the area of Quezaltenango and San Marcos. One is the draw loom, where a draw-boy (or girl) standing at the side of the loom pulls a predetermined sequence of cords, thereby raising the pattern leashes for the weaver, who throws the shuttle. The other, a development of the draw loom, is the jacquard (considered by some to be the forerunner of the computer), which controls individual warp threads through a system of punched cards. Both the draw loom and the jacquard make it possible to weave intricate repeating patterns the length of the fabric with speed and accuracy.

PRINCIPAL TECHNIQUES

With Guatemalan textiles, an understanding of the time-consuming techniques involved in their making adds enormously to the enjoyment of their robust designs.

Many of the items of clothing in this book are made up of rectangular panels of plain or striped material sewn together. Because of the unique way in which the Indian weavers in South, Central and North America mount the warp threads on their back-strap looms, each panel has four selvedges (unless two panels have been woven as one and then cut in half, in which case each panel will have three selvedges and one hemmed edge where the material was cut). These panels are later stitched together to make the *huipils*, shirts, carrying cloths and so on, with no recourse to scissors nor any of the wastage that tailoring entails. Superimposed on prominent areas of

these panels at the time of weaving are wonderful designs — examples of which are illustrated in this book — worked using a variety of different techniques.

By far the largest group falls under the heading of brocades. Brocading is a method of weaving in which thicker, contrasting threads (called supplementary wefts) are inserted in the ground weave, row by row, building up designs in vibrant colours. There are basically three different types of brocading: single-faced, two-faced and double-faced (for details, see glossary). The designs are not drawn on paper but carried in the weaver's head, for she will have been familiar with them all her life, having been taught them as a young girl. Although each individual weaver may put her own interpretation on to her village's customary designs, she is not concerned with originality as we tend to be in the West; rather, she is proud to be following the Maya tradition. There are, however, occasions when quite new motifs are introduced from an outside source. For example, in Chichicastenango and San Antonio Aguas Calientes new motifs with a distinctly European look were introduced in the 1960s. These designs were based on European paper patterns for cross stitch, which the weavers cleverly converted into double-faced brocading (see pp. 38–9, 66–7).

Three further weaving techniques, less widely used, complete the picture. The first is weft wrapping (technically similar to soumak, used in some oriental rugs), which lends itself to more linear designs and can be seen in *huipils* from Colotenango and neighbouring villages (see pp. 24–5). The next is tapestry, a freer form of weaving akin to picture-making, used to weave hair ribbons, particularly in the vicinity of Totonicapán (see pp. 28–9). Lastly, open-work gauze weave which is used in a type of material worn in the Alta Verapaz region in the north, especially in and around Cobán. Here the effect is subtle because only white cotton is used for both warp and weft: it is the open-work weave structure, together with inlay designs, that gives this method its special character.

Embroidery is another way to embellish a textile, and it was, in fact, mistaken by early travellers for brocading. (Superficially, they do look rather similar, but whereas brocading is inserted into the fabric while the panel is being woven, embroidery is added to the finished garment after it is taken off the loom.) Embroidery is found on some *huipils* as the main decorative technique (see pp. 60–61), but it is mostly used in the finish and decorative trim of garments — for example: around the neckline to prevent fraying, in the brightly coloured stitching (*randa*) used to join panels together selvedge to selvedge when making up complete garments (see pp. 26–7), and in certain tailored items of menswear that are embroidered by the men themselves (see pp. 34–5).

Finally, there is the dying technique used for the *jaspe* thread. In this process the design is applied to the threads before they are woven, rather than being added afterwards (see illustration, p.12). The particular characteristic of *jaspe* is the blurred outlines of the design motifs. Two things account for this: first, although the areas of the thread that are to appear white or a contrasting colour in the final cloth are bound up tightly to resist the dye, inevitably a little of the colour creeps underneath the bound areas; and secondly, during the actual process of mounting the warp on the loom (after the ties have been removed), each individual thread moves a little in relation to those on either side of it, so that what started as a straight line, for example, ends up blurred.

Both warp and weft threads can be dyed in this manner and sometimes both are used in the same garment. This is so with some of the skirt materials found around Salcajá, Totonicapán and Quezaltenango, where stripes of plain colour are interspersed with *jaspe* threads in both warp and weft, producing a kind of crazy plaid.

Many *tzutes* are weft-faced, and here it is the weft threads that carry the designs (which are sometimes quite intricate, with someone's name or a greeting spelt out in capital letters). Shawls are often warp-faced and so the designs are in the warp and again alternate with plain-coloured warp stripes (see pp. 30–31, 54–5).

The instantly recognizable material of the women's *huipils* and men's shirts and trousers in Sololá is another example of the combination of plain narrow and *jaspe* warp stripes (see pp. 56–7).

Old-style shirt and trousers from Todos Santos (early 20th century), woven with hand-spun cotton.

PATTERN AND SYMBOLISM

The easiest way to pattern a fabric, seen the world over, is to introduce stripes along the length or bands across the width, or to combine the two to produce checks. Guatemala is no exception, and many towns and villages have a style and colour sequence that identifies the place in which a garment was made. But it does not end there, because superimposed on these striped, plain white or coloured grounds are brocaded patterns and symbols that encode Maya history and pronounce the ethnicity of the wearer.

Some of the designs are abstract and may well have been adopted because the shapes used — triangles, diamonds, lozenges, chevrons, zigzags — lend themselves to the technique of weaving. Even so, symbolism is often attributed to them. For example, vertical zigzags are described as lightning or, as has been suggested by Pettersen (1976, p. 260) in respect of *huipils* from Tamahú and Tactic, 'the winding path the priest has to take up the steep steps of the temple' (see pp. 80–81), while the horizontal 'S' is described as a two-headed snake. Some weavers, though, when approached on this subject, are surprised to be asked what a design means.

Nevertheless, there are many naturalistic symbols among the repertoire of designs based on the flora and fauna of Guatemala (see pp. 60–61), although some may be so abstract that they are not immediately identifiable. Some motifs depict creatures mentioned in the creation myths retold in the *Popol Vuh*, the great Maya testament (see Tedlock 1985), such as lions, jaguars, opossums, dogs and monkeys, as well as double-headed eagles, quetzals, peacocks, owls, bats, turkeys, hens and ducks. Other popular motifs include ceiba trees, pine trees and corn plants.

The double-headed eagle, an image that appears in many parts of the world, was conferred on the Quiché Indian tribe by the Spanish Crown, but was already familiar to them as representing one of the first four men created, according to the Maya myths, or the duality of the gods. A large part of the central

A man's hand-knitted woollen bag from Nahualá. The double-headed eagle motif can be attributed to both European and Maya influence.

panel of the *huipils* from Chichicastenango (1930s to '60s) is taken up by a stylized double-headed eagle (see pp. 32–3). Even the stylization in time becomes so abstract that one could be forgiven for not recognizing the bold horizontal zigzags covering most of the *huipil* as wing and tail feathers — all that remains of the original eagle. The double-headed eagle also appears on *huipils* from Chuarrancho (see p. 75) and various textiles from Nahualá.

Another form of symbolism can be found on the same earlier *huipils* from Chichicastenango (pp. 32–3). If the three-panel garment is laid out flat and viewed as a whole, it will be seen that the brocaded areas form a cross; the silk appliqué points surrounding

the hole cut for the head represent the sun, and the four small silk roundels appliquéd to the front, back and two shoulders represent the four cardinal points — North, South, East and West — that are central to Maya beliefs. The sun is also embroidered on the flaps of the men's tailored woollen short trousers from Chichicastenango. According to Pettersen (1976, p. 92), three designs on these flaps (which, incidentally, have no practical use) indicate the wearer's position in society as boy, young man or elder. The elaborateness of the chain-stitching in which the motifs are worked increases with each stage in life.

In Nebaj, the largest of a group of isolated villages in the Cuchumatánes mountains, the iconography of the textiles is based on a folk narrative. A visitor from Nebaj related the story to me while staying in my home: A beautiful girl falls in love with a young man of whom her father disapproves, and turns him into a bird so that he can fly up and visit her in her room, but the girl's father discovers this trick and the young couple flee on horseback. The bold designs appearing on these *huipils*, *tzutes* and wide hairbands include a bird, human figures and a horse (all the same height). The weft-faced motifs are brocaded in a bold lacing technique only found in Nebaj and two neighbouring villages (see pp. 44–5).

The peace (or so it would seem to the visitor) of the villages that lie on the shores of Lake Atitlán produces textiles with an altogether lighter touch. There are *huipils* with rows of tiny polychrome ducks and dogs

(San Lucas Tolimán), charming birds and butterflies embroidered in primary colours on a white ground (San Pablo La Laguna; see p. 60), and slightly larger birds of every description embroidered on trouser legs, superimposed on dark purple and white stripes (Santiago Atitlán).

The human figure, too, is often depicted in an amusing manner, with outline shapes reminiscent of the rows of paper dolls that children cut out from folded sheets of paper. On a *tzute* from Chichicastenango four large doll-like figures horizontally striped in yellow, orange and green fill the whole area (see pp. 40–41). In a *jaspe* shawl from San Cristóbal Totonicapán, if one looks carefully into the narrow stripes, among the other motifs one can find twin dolls squeezed between pine trees above and corn plants below (see p. 30).

TRADITION AND CHANGE

Certain elements of Guatemalan costume have remained unchanged since the beginning of the first millennium. If one studies the wall paintings, stone reliefs, figures on pots and figurines of pre-Columbian sites, it appears that at that time clothes were made from rectangles of material woven on the back-strap loom, as many still are today. Women are portrayed wearing a length of material wrapped around the waist and held in position by a sash or belt; panels are shown joined together, with a hole or slit for the head, forming a *huipil*; and hair is elaborately dressed. For men, a few basic items worn then — cape, hip cloth and sandals — have survived in some places in modern-day dress. Simple clothes such as these were augmented after the Conquest by cut and tailored garments, for example the red jacket worn until recently by Ixil-speaking Indians in Nebaj, Chajul and San Juan Cotzal (see p. 49), or the distinctive jacket and knee-length trousers of Chichicastenango. Women also adopted new styles in Cobán and Quezaltenango, preferring fully gathered skirts to wrap-around *cortes*.

But this was in the past, and now it is necessary to look at what has happened in recent times. Twenty years of guerrilla warfare have brought about profound changes. At a time when all male Indians' activities were suspect, it was no longer advisable to draw

Brocaded motif of a doll-like figure on an all-purpose cloth from Chichicastenango (see also pp. 40–41).

attention to oneself by wearing village-specific clothing. At the same time, North American imports of shirts and trousers available in the markets were cheaper than hand-woven clothes.

Today traditional male dress is mostly worn only on special occasions and in connection with *cofradía* activities. Yet even the traditional place which the Catholic religion has always held in the community is under threat: evangelical movements are moving in, making significant numbers of converts and thereby eroding long-held traditions of family life. Sadly, these missionaries consider that wearing traditional costume is inappropriate and persuade the women who join them to abandon *traje*.

On the other hand, the horrors of the 1980s — described by Coe (1993, p. 212) as 'ethnocide' — have, paradoxically, strengthened the resolve of Maya groups in their stand to be recognized. The publication in 1984 of Rigoberta Menchu's personal story describing this ethnocide as it affected her and her family, and her subsequent award of the Nobel Peace Prize in 1992, has for the first time brought the plight of the Maya to the attention of the world.

Greater interest in the Maya has in turn stimulated the trade in crafts. Many beautiful hand-woven products can be bought from dealers and found in specialist shops and co-operatives, but it must be said that a large proportion of the goods on sale in popular tourist centres such as Antigua, Panajachel and Chichicastenango are mass-produced. It would be impossible to sustain the volume of goods for sale if this were not the case.

Meanwhile, women still weaving on their back-strap looms not only pursue their interpretations of traditional clothes using new colours and yarns, but maintain or even revive designs from the past with a new sense of pride. With the advent of better schooling and improved communications, younger women are also taking an interest in the indigenous costumes of other towns, and are not above wearing an alternative *huipil* to their own if they admire it. As do the young the world over, they also follow fashion, embracing new ideas and rejecting old. I was in Santiago Atitlán on Good Friday in 1999, a day when everyone was in the main square dressed in their best attire, and saw only one old woman wearing the traditional 8 m (26 ft) long red ribbon, which, when wrapped around the head, stands out 3–4 cm (about 1–1½ in) like a halo (see top photograph, p. 9). Open any book on Guatemalan costume and turn up the page for Santiago Atitlán, and you are sure to see this unusual headgear being worn by everyone in the picture. Not any more!

Literature on Guatemalan textiles from the 1930s onwards has been predicting their imminent decline, and the foregoing paragraphs have indicated the dangers. But the new sense of cultural identity, coupled with the cross-fertilization of ideas that is taking place, would seem to suggest that these prophets of doom are mistaken.

MEXICO

HUEHUETENANGO

THE CUCHUMATANE

Todos Santos Cuchumatán

Colotenango

Huehuetenango

Chajul

Nebaj

San Juan Cotzal

EL QUICHÉ

ALTA VERAPAZ

Cobán

San Cristóbal
Verapaz

Tactic

Tamahú

**SAN
MARCOS**

San Marcos

Momostenango

TOTONICAPÁN

San Cristóbal
Totonicapán

Salcajá

Quezaltenango

Cantel

Santa Cruz
del Quiché

Zacualpa

Chichicastenango

Salamá

BAJA VERAPAZ

Totonicapán

Nahualá

Sololá

SOLOLÁ

San Pablo
La Laguna

L. Atitlán

S

Santiago
Atitlán

San Lucas
Tolimán

Panajachel

Tecpán

CHIMALTENANGO

Chuarrancho

San Raimundo

EL PROGRESO

El Progreso

GUATEMALA

Jalapa

Chimaltenango

San Antonio
Aguas Calientes

Antigua

Santa Maria de Jesús

Guatemala City

JALAPA

QUEZALTENANGO

Retalhuleu

Mazatenango

SACATEPÉQUEZ

RETALHULEU

SUCHITEPÉQUEZ

Escuintla

Cuilapa

ESCUINTLA

SANTA ROSA

PACIFIC OCEAN

◆ department capital
• town / village

Inset map:

USA

*ATLANTIC
OCEAN*

Gulf of Mexico

BAHAMAS

MEXICO

CUBA

JAMAICA

DOMINICAN
REPUBLIC

HAITI

BELIZE

HONDURAS

Caribbean Sea

GUATEMALA

EL SALVADOR

NICARAGUA

COSTA RICA

PANAMA

*PACIFIC
OCEAN*

VENEZUELA

COLOMBIA

HUIPIL
Three-panel *huipil* with a loose collar,
made from red and white cotton cloth woven
with hand-spun yarn on a back-strap loom.

Narrow red warps are crossed with wide
bands of red brocading, with touches of
other colours. The attached collar is
decorated with blue rickrack.
89 × 81 cm (35 × 32 in)

CROSSING COLOURED WARPS AND WEFTS
TO FORM CHECKS IS ONE OF THE SIMPLEST
METHODS OF BRINGING INTEREST TO A
WOVEN TEXTILE. ONLY USING IT IN PART,
AS HERE, IS UNUSUAL. THE FRILLY COLLAR
AND ITS BLUE POMPOMS CONTRAST WITH
THE FORMALITY OF THE RED PANEL AND
CHECK STRIPING.

HUIPIL
Huipil made from three four-selvedge
panels sewn together.

Dense, single-faced brocaded areas
are superimposed on red and white stripes.
Various weft-wrapping techniques (similar
to soumak) have been used. Other villages
close by produce similar textiles.
53 × 103 cm (21 × 40½ in)

BY LEAVING GAPS IN THE BANDS OF RED
BROCADING, THE WHITE STRIPES OF THE
FOUNDATION CLOTH APPEAR AS DOTS. THE
SMALL VERTICAL BARS AND INTRICATE
DESIGNS IN SQUARES MAKE A LIVELY ADDITION.

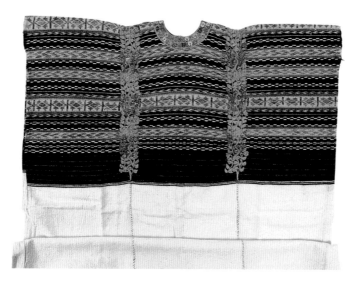

HUIPIL
A woman's *huipil* made from three
weft-faced panels sewn together.

Bands of *jaspe* patterns (dark blue and white) and
supplementary weft patterning (mauve and yellow)
decorate the upper part of the garment. The plain white
portion underneath is tucked into the skirt.
106.5 × 120.5 cm (42 × 47 in)

THE DETAIL ILLUSTRATIONS SHOW A SPLENDID EMBROIDERED
RANDA THAT COVERS THE SEAM JOINING TWO OF THE PANELS,
DEPICTING LEAVES AND FLOWERS EITHER SIDE OF A TWISTING
STEM, AND A DELICATELY EMBROIDERED NECK OPENING THAT
INTRODUCES A CONTRASTING TOUCH OF NATURALISTIC COLOUR.

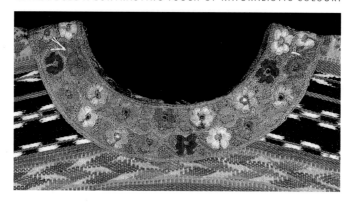

HAIR RIBBON

Long ribbons (*cintas*)
are wound into the hair in
many towns and villages.

These tapestry-woven
ribbons, in silk, cotton or
rayon, are finished with
pompoms connected by
wire-wrapped maguey
loops, ending in long
tassels. Laid out side
by side (right) are
different sections.
3.5 × 350 cm
(1⅜ in × 11 ft 6 in)

THERE IS A STRUCTURE TO
THE ALL-OVER DESIGN OF
THE RIBBON THAT DERIVES
FROM THE FORMAL BANDS OF
COLOUR SEPARATING FIGUR-
ATIVE AND ABSTRACT FORMS.

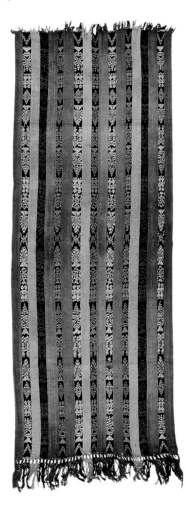

THE *JASPE* STRIPE (LEFT) SHOWS TYPICAL PATTERNS USED IN TIE-DYED WARPS — FOR EXAMPLE, THE TWIN FIGURES AND A PINE TREE. THE BLURRED EDGES TO THE DESIGNS ARE AN INHERENT PART OF THE IKAT PROCESS.

CEREMONIAL SHAWL
or *perraje*, which is worn either over
the shoulder or as a wrap.

Wide bands of muted coloured silk
alternate with bands of hand-spun cotton
jaspe thread. The knotted fringe shows
considerable signs of wear.
72 × 188 cm (28⅓ in × 6 ft 2 in)

HUIPIL

A *huipil* made of three four-selvedge
panels of brown cotton, brocaded on
the front, back and shoulders.

The design on the central panel
represents the double-headed eagle
(symbolizing the double-headed deity);
the horizontal bars represent its
wing and tail feathers.
66 × 89 cm (26 × 35 in)

IF THE *HUIPIL* IS LAID OUT FLAT,
THE SYMBOLISM OF THE DESIGN
AS A WHOLE CAN BE SEEN. THE
BRAIDED AREAS BACK AND
FRONT FORM A CROSS; THE
NECK OPENING WITH ITS SILK

APPLIQUÉ OF RADIATING POINTS
REPRESENTS THE SUN, AND THE
FOUR ROSETTES REPRESENT THE
FOUR PHASES OF THE MOON OR
THE CARDINAL POINTS: NORTH,
SOUTH, EAST AND WEST.

JACKET AND TROUSERS

The simply shaped jacket and unusually shaped short
trousers are thought to be based on archaic Spanish costume.

They are cut and tailored from black woollen twill cloth.
A short black woollen fringe on the back of the jacket is covered
with silk cords knotted into the fabric. The knee-length trousers
have a decorated flap on each side, caught in the waistband.
Jacket: 56 cm (22 in) across shoulders; length 51 cm (20 in)
Trousers: 33 cm (13 in) across waist; length 66 cm (26 in)

THE STEM OF EACH FLOWER EMBROIDERED ON THE BACK OF THE JACKET FOLLOWS THE CURVE OF THE SCROLL. THE DETAIL ALSO SHOWS PART OF THE BLUE ZIGZAG LINE IN CHAIN STITCH THAT DECORATES EACH SHOULDER.

IT IS SAID THAT THE AMOUNT AND CONTENT OF THE CHAIN-STITCH EMBROIDERY SEWN BY THE MEN ON TO THE FLAPS OF THEIR TROUSERS INDICATES THEIR STANDING IN LIFE — WHETHER YOUTH, ADULT OR ELDER.

HUIPIL
Huipil made up of three four-selvedge panels
of brown cotton, brocaded on the front, back and
shoulders, with a velvet trim neckline.

The wings and tail feathers of the double-headed
eagle on the central panel are represented by
chevrons, a feature repeated and
exaggerated on the side panels.
70 × 81 cm (27 ½ × 32 in)

DETAIL OF THE CHEVRON AREA
OF THIS DESIGN SHOWS THAT
IT IS POSSIBLE EVEN WHEN
USING NUMEROUS VIBRANT
HUES TO ACHIEVE A HARMONY
BY CAREFULLY PLACING
EACH COLOUR BESIDE A
COMPLEMENTARY COLOUR.

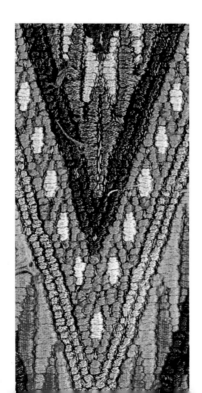

HUIPIL
Three-panel, four-selvedge brown cotton
huipil brocaded in purple and pink silk floss and
brightly coloured stranded cottons.

The stylized eagle of the previous two *huipils*
has given way to exuberant roses, converted from
printed cross-stitch patterns to the typical raised
brocading technique of Chichicastenango.
66 × 100 cm (26 × 39⅓ in)

THE BOLD TWIST MOTIF
PROVIDES A FOCAL POINT
ON THE TWO SIDE PANELS.
THIS, TOGETHER WITH THE
STRIPED VERTICAL BARS OF
THE *RANDAS*, CONTRASTS
THE ABSTRACT WITH THE
NATURALISTIC ELEMENTS OF
THE DESIGN.

TZUTE
Rectangular cloth used
as a head-cloth, shawl or cover

Originally woven in one long piece on the
back-strap loom, it was subsequently cut in half
and the pieces sewn together side by side, with
the fringes aligned at one end and the
raw edges hemmed at the other.
70 × 63.5 cm (27 ½ × 25 in)

THE WEAVER'S PERSONAL ADAPTATION OF THE POPULAR
DOLL FIGURE HAS BEEN TREATED IN A BOLD WAY.
YELLOW, ORANGE AND GREEN ACRYLICS HAVE BEEN USED
FOR THE DOUBLE-FACED BROCADING OVER THE RED AND
ORANGE STRIPED GROUND.

40

COFRADÍA HEADDRESS
Man's triangular scarf, worn with
the two ends tied at the nape of the neck

It is initially woven as one rectangular piece (twice as long
as wide), which is cut in two diagonally from a point halfway down one
side. The smaller piece, turned through an angle of 180 degrees, is abutted to
the larger one and the two selvedges joined with a *randa* to form a triangle.
152.5 cm / 60 in (top edge) × 99 cm / 39 in (sides)

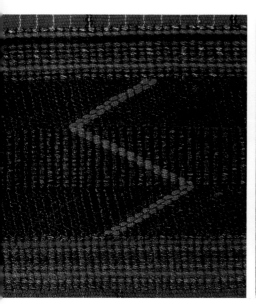

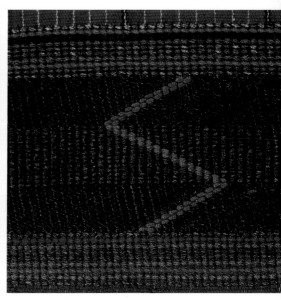

THE RESTRAINED, MINIMAL DESIGN ELEMENTS ENTIRELY RESTRICTED TO
THE BORDER (WORKED IN SOUMAK), THE SELVEDGES AND THE *RANDA*
MAKE FOR A VERY STRIKING COLOUR SCHEME. A SINGLE ORNAMENT HAS
BEEN ATTACHED TO ONE OF THE STRANDS OF THE LARGE TASSEL.

HERE THE IMAGERY IS DRAWN FROM A FOLK NARRATIVE (SEE P. 18). BECAUSE THE DESIGN IS WOVEN IN SINGLE-FACED BROCADING, WHERE NOTHING SHOWS ON THE REVERSE OF THE FABRIC, IT IS ALSO POSSIBLE TO ADMIRE THE CAREFUL ARRANGEMENT OF COLOURS IN THE STRIPED GROUND FABRIC (SEE OVERLEAF).

FRINGED CLOTH (*TZUTE*)

Women wore this type of all-purpose cloth folded on the head during *cofradía* ceremonies.

Made from a single striped panel, the *tzute* is almost completely covered with rich brocading. The ends are finished with decorative machine stitching in white cotton, with the warp ends left as fringes.
75 cm (29½ in) square, excluding fringes

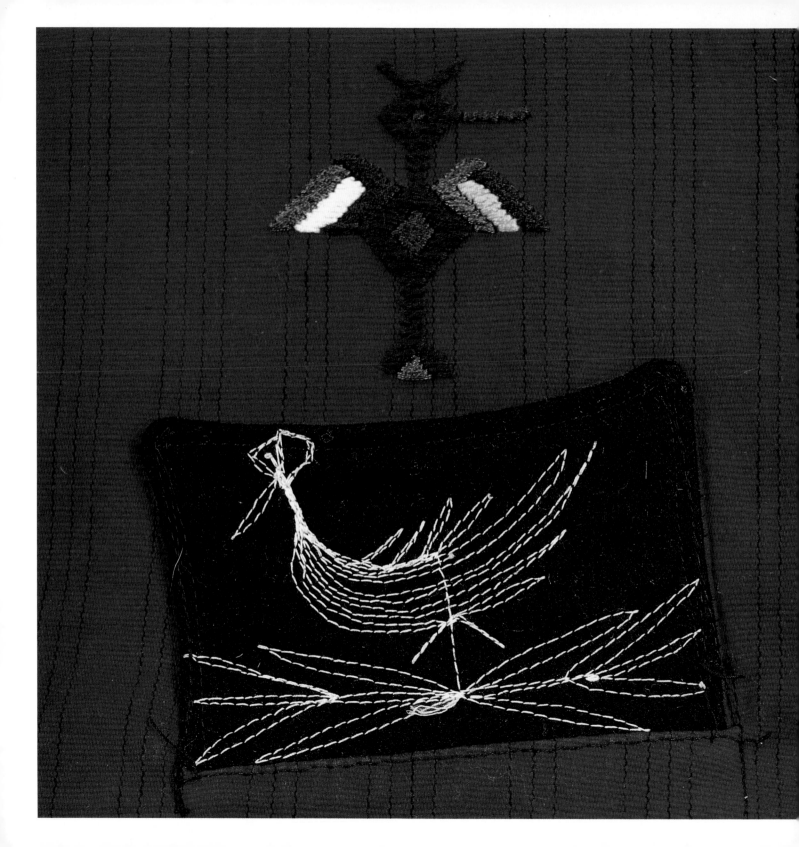

MAN'S JACKET
Showing European influence, the jacket
is tailored in red cotton and lined throughout.
The lapels and cuffs are faced with black material,
and black braid is used on the front and back.

In all three Ixil villages — Nebaj, Chajul and San
Juan Cotzal — men used to wear red jackets similar
to this, but they are seldom seen today.
53 cm (21 in) across chest
71 cm (28 in) neck to hem

[OPPOSITE] A SINGLE BIRD IN PROFILE HOVERS OVER THE
LIVELY MACHINE-STITCHED BIRD ON THE BREAST POCKET.
THE OTHER TWO POCKETS ARE DECORATED WITH BRAID.

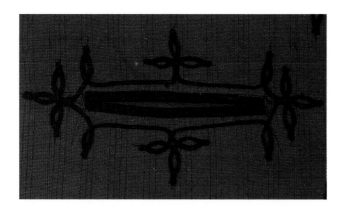

[OPPOSITE] DETAIL OF
THE SWIRL OF BRAID
ON THE SLEEVE WHERE
IT MEETS THE BLACK
CUFF, WHICH IS DEC-
ORATED WITH MACHINE
STITCHING.

DETAIL OF THE BACK
OF THE GARMENT,
SHOWING RANDOMLY
PLACED BIRD MOTIFS
AND AN UNIDENTIFIED
OBJECT.

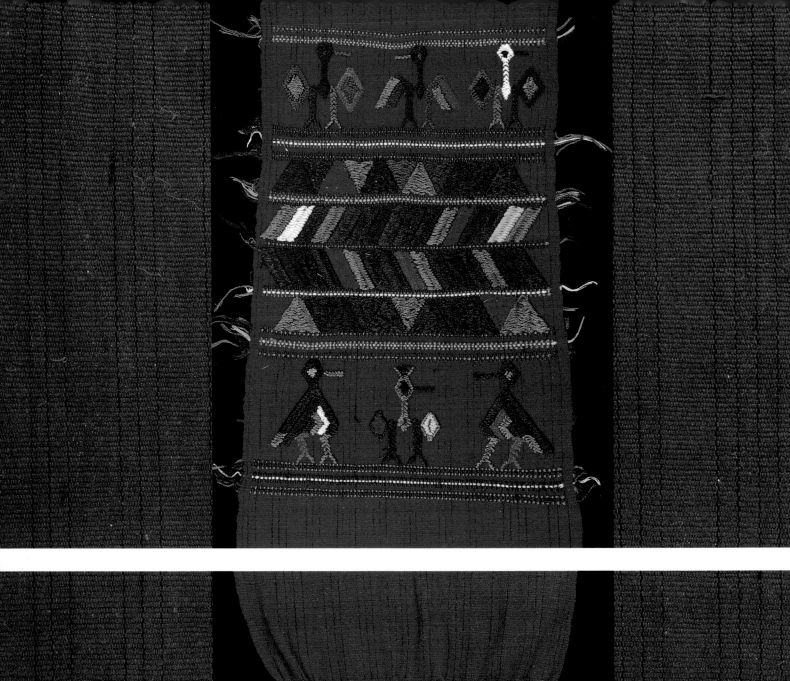

MAN'S SASH
Long red band with chevron and
zoomorphic designs, worn around the waist.

The brocaded design is woven on a red cotton ground striped
with fine black lines. The occasional bands of supplementary weft
between the designs are extended to both sides, leaving tufts
of yarn. The red and black warp ends are gathered
into thick plaits ending in pompoms.
26.5 × 334 cm (10 ½ in × 11 ft)

IN THESE LAST FEW EXAMPLES THE REPRESENTATION OF BIRDS
APPEARS TO THE EUROPEAN EYE TO HAVE BECOME SO STYLIZED
AND SO FAR REMOVED FROM ANY ATTEMPT TO REFLECT THEIR
NATURAL COLOURING THAT THEY BECOME PURELY DECORATIVE.
[OPPOSITE] THE BACKGROUND FABRIC OF BRILLIANT RED, WITH A
REGULAR DIVISION OF FINE BLACK LINES, LENDS A RICHNESS TO
THE DEEP COLOURS OF THE BROCADED MOTIFS.

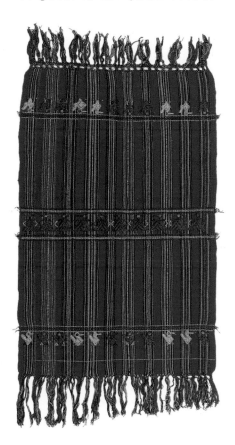

THE PROMINENT RED OF THE
WARP STRIPES CONTRASTS
BOLDLY WITH THE GREENS
OF THE BROCADING.

RED COTTON CLOTH
A shawl (*perraje*) or all-purpose cloth
of red cotton striped with many vibrant colours,
with knotted fringes at each end.

Three bands of brocaded birds are contained within
narrow bands of supplementary weft, which extend in little
tufts similar to those on the Chajul sash (see pp. 52–3).
77 × 52 cm (30¼ × 20½ in) excluding fringe

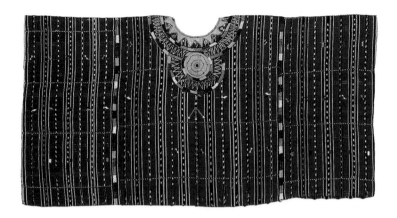

COFRADÍA HUIPIL
A special three-panel garment worn over the everyday
huipil, sometimes referred to as a *sobrehuipil*.

The defining feature of the Sololá costume for both men
and women is the narrow *jaspe* stripes (usually black and white)
alternating with the red stripes of the ground weave.
72 × 138 cm (28⅓ in × 54 in)

[OPPOSITE] PINK SATIN IS APPLIQUÉD TO THE NECK IN THE FORM
OF RADIATING POINTS, WITH A ROSETTE OF THE SAME MATERIAL
POSITIONED UNDERNEATH.

THE COLOUR OF THE BLOCKS
IN THE TWO *RANDAS* JOIN-
ING THE PANELS TOGETHER
IS ECHOED IN STITCHING IN
THE SAME COLOURS AROUND
THE APPLIQUÉ MOTIFS.

EMBROIDERED *HUIPIL*

White two-panel *huipil* with widely spaced lines
using multiple wefts. The *huipil* is embroidered in
primary colours and has an attached muslin collar.

Lake Atitlán, in its idyllic setting at the foot
of three volcanoes, acts as a magnet to visitors to
Guatemala. The butterflies and ducks embroidered on
this *huipil*, as well as the flowers on the collar, recreate
the flora and fauna of the surroundings.
76 × 74 cm (30 × 29 in)

(OPPOSITE) THE RUFFLED
MUSLIN COLLAR, MADE OF
LIGHTER MATERIAL THAN
THE *HUIPIL*, IS DECORATED
WITH A WIDE FLORAL BAND
EDGED WITH A VIVID RED.

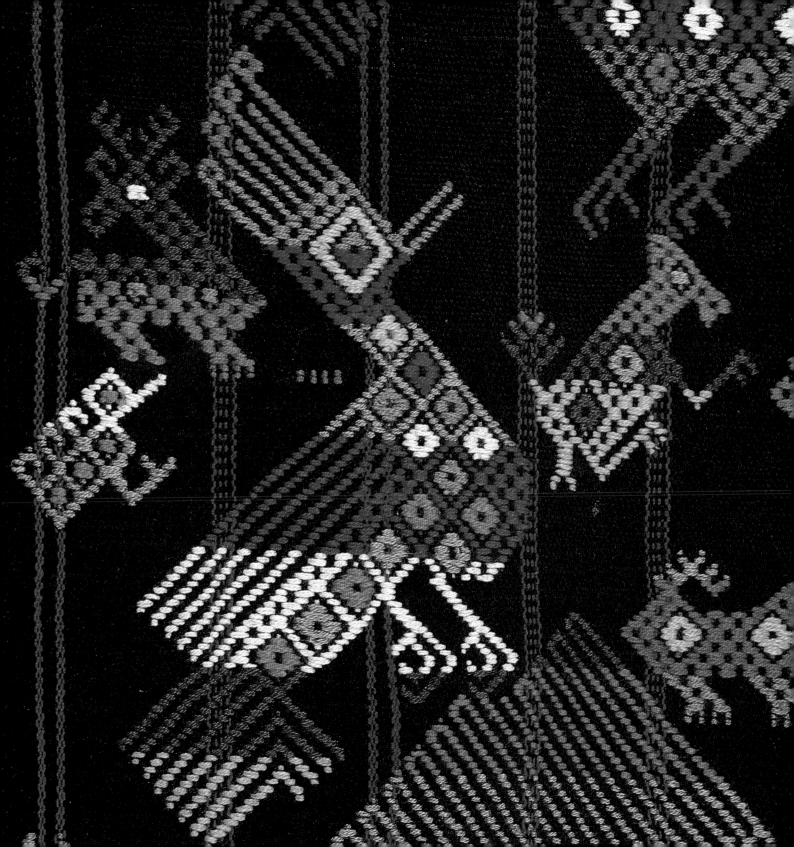

THIS WOVEN PATTERN SHOWS
ALL THE SIGNS OF HAVING BEEN
DESIGNED ON A MATRIX BUT IN
FACT EXPLOITS THE 'STEP AND
REPEAT' OF TWILL LINES. THIS,
TOGETHER WITH THE FREQUENT
CHANGES OF COLOUR, MAKES
FOR A STRONG DESIGN.

FRINGED *TZUTE*

Part of the men's costume, displaying
zoomorphic motifs of exotic birds and animals
within a frame of diamond frets.

Made from a single cotton panel of
indigo-dyed ground with pairs of magenta warp-
way stripes at intervals. The orange fringes have
been knotted into the ends of the cloth.
75 × 61 cm (29 ½ × 24 in)
excluding fringes

HUIPIL
Two views of a simple, white
cotton *huipil*. The front (above) shows jaguars, the
back (right) lines up splendid peacocks surrounded
by little birds.

There are some signs that the colour has run,
but this is of no consequence to the women —
who sometimes actively encourage it.
74 × 96.5 cm (29 × 38 in)

THE TWO ELEMENTS OF THE DESIGN, THE BORDER
AND THE ANIMAL/BIRD MOTIFS, ARE UNITED BY
THE USE OF DIAMONDS, INFILLED WITH COLOUR.
THIS IS A FEATURE OF TEXTILES FROM NAHUALÁ.

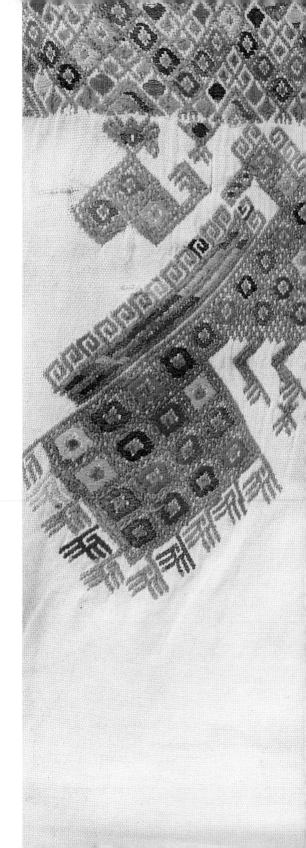

64

TZUTE

Two-panel cloth worn folded on the head
or used as a utility cloth.

Weavers in this village are generally
acknowledged for their weaving expertise.
The motifs on the red ground between the striped
selvedges are worked in double-faced brocading,
a technique that resembles tapestry.
76 × 105 cm (30 × 41 in)

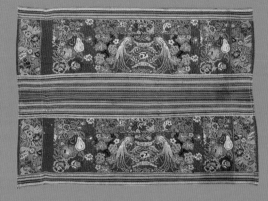

THE DESIGNS IN SAN ANTONIO CHANGED IN THE
1960s WHEN WESTERN PATTERNS FOR CROSS
STITCH APPEARED. THE COMPLEXITY OF THE
SELVEDGES (STRIPES) CONTRASTS STRIKINGLY WITH
THE REALISM OF THE BIRDS, FISHES AND FRUIT.

HUIPIL
Beautifully woven two-panel, four-selvedge *huipil*
from San Antonio Aguas Calientes, displaying the many
different designs in the weaver's repertoire.

The figurative band is reserved for the part
that falls on to the shoulder. The non-figurative
bands, worked in a virtuoso display of different
techniques, use stranded brocading
threads in a large range of colours.
57 × 67 cm (22½ × 26⅓ in)

THE USE OF A KALEIDOSCOPE OF COLOURS (EACH
REQUIRING A SEPARATE BROCADING THREAD), IS
PULLED TOGETHER VISUALLY BY THE MICROSCOPIC
APPEARANCE OF THE RED BINDING ENDS OF THE
WARP OVERLAYING THE BRIGHT COLOURS.

HUIPIL
Two-panel *huipil* in distinctively coloured
stripes of mauve, red, pale yellow and hand-spun
natural brown cotton overlaid with exotic motifs.

Thick stranded threads are brocaded on a closed warp, giving
two faces — positive on the front and negative on the back. There are
similarities in colour and style with textiles from San Juan Sacatepéquez
nearby. Both show fantastic creatures above, and below a motif
variously called the 'feathered serpent' or 'rolling hills'.
66 × 109 cm (26 × 43 in)

THE STRENGTH OF THE
BROCADING COMBINES
TRIUMPHANTLY WITH
THE BOLD WARP STRIPES
— TO STUNNING EFFECT.

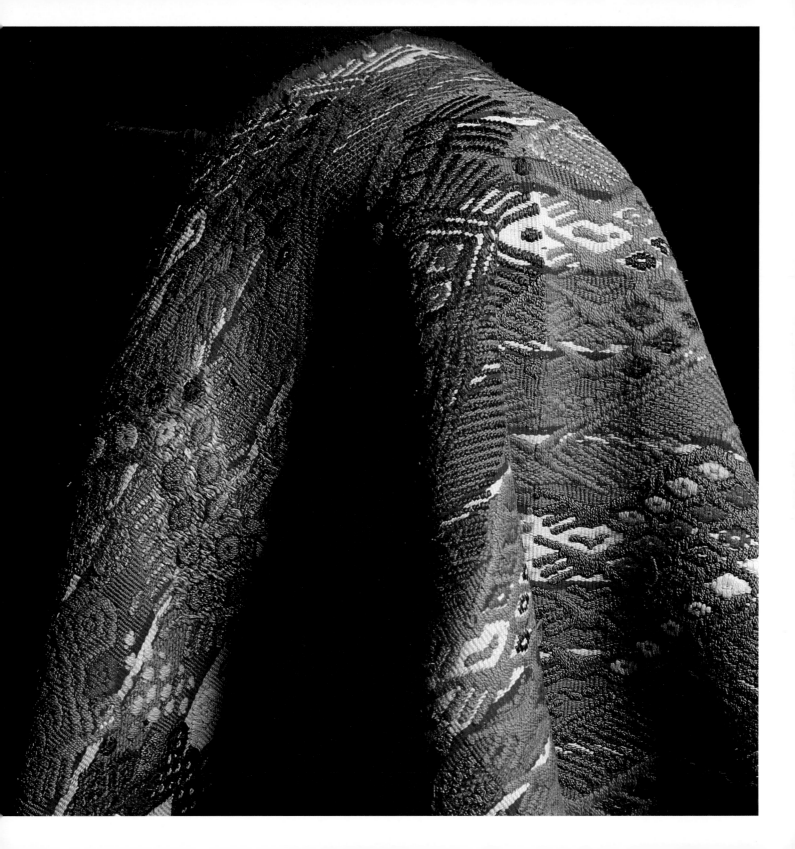

THE DEAD-TURKEY MOTIF (SHOWN OPPOSITE) IS A FEATURE OF TEXTILES
FROM SAN RAIMUNDO, SAN JUAN AND SAN PEDRO SACATEPÉQUEZ.

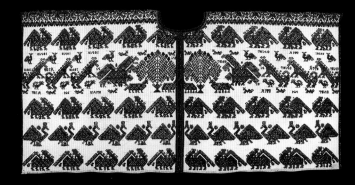

CEREMONIAL *HUIPIL*
This large two-panel ceremonial garment is
worn loose over the everyday *huipil*.

Three strands of brocading thread are used
for the looped-pile method of brocading, giving a
density to each individual motif and adding
weight to the finished garment.
68 × 128 cm (26¾ × 50 in)

THE RESTRAINED USE
OF THE RUST COLOUR
IN AN OTHERWISE
MONOCHROME DESIGN
IS A CONSTANT SUR-
PRISE — AS IN THIS
PEACOCK MOTIF.

TWO OBJECTS THAT
ARE OF SYMBOLIC
SIGNIFICANCE TO THE
MAYA ARE FEATURED
IN THIS *HUIPIL*: THE
CEIBA TREE AND THE
COYOTE.

HUIPIL

An unused two-panel white *huipil* brocaded in dark purple
and red. The neck edge is oversewn with emerald green.

The central design motif is the double-headed eagle
separated by corn plants. The rest of the field is filled with rows of rabbits,
opossums and birds. The ends of the brocading threads, which have
been carefully woven in, appear as faint dots.

57 × 105 cm (22½ × 41 in)

THE ARRANGEMENT OF
THE CENTRAL PANEL AND
SHOULDER BROCADING,
AS WELL AS THE APPARENT
ARBITRARINESS OF THE

INTERSECTING NARROW
RED BANDS, IS ENHANCED
BY THE STARK SIMPLICITY
OF THE COLOURING,

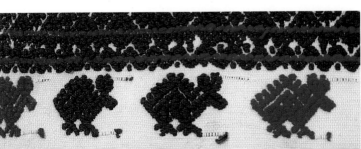

UNCUT *HUIPIL*

Unfinished three-panel *huipil* in which the two
white panels are slightly longer than the red. The hole
for the head has yet to be cut out.

There are three Pocomchi villages — Cristóbal,
Tactic, and Tamahú — whose *huipils* are to a certain extent
interchangeable. The palette of this *huipil*, restricted to
red, green and yellow, is particularly satisfying.
40 (43) × 102 cm (15¾ [17] × 40 in)

THE BORDERS ABOVE AND
BELOW THE ZIGZAG DISPLAY
THE BIRD-ON-TOP-OF-TREE
MOTIF. THE DENSITY OF THE
RED PANEL ACTS AS A FOIL
TO THE SIMPLICITY OF THE

WHITE PANELS WITH THEIR
DIAMOND MOTIF COMPOSED
OF SIXTEEN SMALL SQUARES
ALTERNATING WITH A 'VASE'-
TYPE MOTIF OF INVERTED
TRIANGLES.

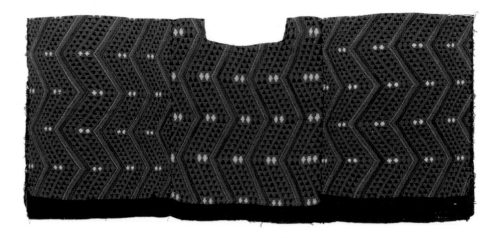

HUIPIL
The three panels of this everyday *huipil*
were woven separately, each with four selvedges.

The dark indigo ground, with its predominantly red
brocading, plays an important part in the decoration.
The dark triangles that follow the zigzag path of the
mauve and green lines (which at first glance
appear to be an addition) are actually the
ground weave, left unbrocaded.
43 × 101 cm (17 × 39¾ in)

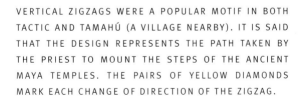

VERTICAL ZIGZAGS WERE A POPULAR MOTIF IN BOTH
TACTIC AND TAMAHÚ (A VILLAGE NEARBY). IT IS SAID
THAT THE DESIGN REPRESENTS THE PATH TAKEN BY
THE PRIEST TO MOUNT THE STEPS OF THE ANCIENT
MAYA TEMPLES. THE PAIRS OF YELLOW DIAMONDS
MARK EACH CHANGE OF DIRECTION OF THE ZIGZAG.

glossary

acrylics synthetic yarns

agave see **maguey**

back-strap loom simple portable loom traditionally used by women in various parts of the world since earliest times. The WARP is spread out on two rods, and tensioned between the weight of the woman's body at one end and a fixed point (on a post or tree) at the other. Also known as a hip loom, body-tensioned loom or stick loom.

binding ends WARP threads that tie down the brocading thread at regular intervals

body-tensioned loom see BACK-STRAP LOOM

brocading method of producing designs with a supplementary WEFT. The thicker, contrasting thread skips over several warps at a time, standing out from the GROUND WEAVE (or background). See also SINGLE-FACED BROCADING, TWO-FACED BROCADING, DOUBLE-FACED BROCADING.

ceiba tall, straight tree of the bombax family (*Bombacaceae*), sacred to the Maya

cellulose the main constituent of plant cell walls, used in the manufacture of rayon

cinta (de pelo) a hair ribbon

cloth beam the beam on which woven cloth is wound, located at the front of a TREADLE LOOM

cofradías religious brotherhoods with both church and civil responsibilities

corte length of material for a skirt

costumbre a custom or tradition (in the context of this book, especially in relation to *COFRADÍAS*)

double-faced brocading brocaded designs that are the same on both sides of the fabric

draw loom special type of loom that increases the capacity for weaving figured fabrics

four-selvedge panel woven panel made to the exact size required, with selvedges at top and bottom as well as at each side

four-shaft treadle loom see TREADLE LOOM

gauze loose-weave fabric in which pairs of WARP threads twisted around each other are held in place by the WEFT

ground weave the foundation fabric of interlaced WARP and WEFT threads on which a design is worked

heddle loop for raising warp thread, string or wire heddles, each containing an eye, are suspended on SHAFTS. See HEDDLE ROD for a simpler device used on BACK-STRAP LOOM.

heddle rod one of the two rods on a loom that are used to separate the WARP into even and uneven threads, which lifts every other warp thread lying under the SHED ROD. A continuous length of yarn is taken alternately under each thread and over the heddle rod across the whole width of the textile, enabling all the alternate threads to be raised as one and the WEFT to be passed through the SHED.

hip loom see BACK-STRAP LOOM

huipil (pronounced 'weepil') simple blouse worn by Maya women, often brocaded or embroidered on the upper part

ikat see *jaspe*

indigo blue dye obtained from various plants of the genus *Indigofera*; but can also refer to the synthetic indigo dye

jaspe resist-dyed threads. WARP or WEFT threads are stretched out under tension and areas that are to remain white (or original colour) are bound up with twine before dyeing. The binding is removed after the dye has been applied, thus revealing the *jaspe* designs.

lacing form of brocading in which the SUPPLEMENTARY WEFT is passed twice in between each throw of the foundation weft

leashes heddles on a DRAW LOOM

maguey tropical plants of the *Agave* family; can also refer to the fibres extracted from their fleshy leaves

perraje shawl or wrap

plaid checks made by crossing coloured stripes in WARP and WEFT

quetzal Central American bird (*Pharomachrus mocinno*) known for its brilliant colours, especially on the male's tail feathers; now an endangered species

raised where the BROCADING thread is lifted slightly between the BINDING ENDS, by a flick of the finger, to give an uncut pile effect

randa decorative stitch worked in a variety of colours to join two panels selvedge to selvedge; featured on skirts, *huipils* and various cloths

shafts slats of wood on a TREADLE LOOM that support the heddles. Each WARP is threaded through the eye of a HEDDLE. Most looms have four shafts.

shed on a loom, the opening made between two layers of WARP threads, through which the shuttle is passed

shed rod one of the two rods on a loom that are used to separate the WARP into even and uneven threads. One set of threads lies over the shed rod, leaving a space in front of it into which to pass the WEFT. To lift the other set of threads with the HEDDLE ROD, the shed rod has to be pushed back along the warp.

single-faced brocading BROCADING in which the design appears on the face of the fabric only

sobrehuipil larger *huipil* worn as an overgarment on top of the everyday one, especially on ceremonial occasions

soumak decorative weaving technique whereby WEFTS are wrapped around WARPS (instead of being interlaced with them), which produces a surface texture similar to chain stitch

stick loom see BACK-STRAP LOOM

supplementary weft contrasting thread additional to the GROUND WEAVE, used in many designs

tapestry WEFT-faced fabric built up of many areas of colour to form a pattern or picture

traje traditional costume

treadle loom sturdy foot-operated floor loom with SHAFTS for raising and lowering the threads. The shafts are attached to treadles, which increases the speed of weaving, compared with the BACK-STRAP LOOM

two-faced brocading technique whereby the design on the face of a fabric appears in negative on the reverse; work produced by this technique

tzute (pronounced 'shoot') term used for a variety of rectangular cloths, such as head-cloths, serviettes and all-purpose carrying cloths

warp threads that lie lengthways in a fabric

warp beam beam on which the WARP is wound, located at the back of a TREADLE LOOM

warp-faced term describing a fabric in which the WARP threads lie so close together that they cover the WEFT

warping process of preparing the WARP threads by measuring off the number and length of threads needed, while winding the thread in a figure-of-eight motion around two or more posts. At the point where they cross, the threads are secured with a length of yarn before being removed from the posts to keep them in the order in which they were wound.

weft transverse threads that interlace with the WARP

weft-faced term describing a fabric in which the WEFT completely covers the WARP

selected reading

The Maya Civilization

Coe, M., *The Maya*, London, 1993. Historical introduction to the Maya, constantly revised and expanded.

McEwan, C., *Ancient Mexico in the British Museum*, London, 1994. Introductory catalogue published to celebrate the new permanent Mexican Gallery, illustrating Aztec and Maya artefacts.

Miller, M., *The Art of Mesoamerica from Olmec to Aztec*, London and New York, 1996. Expert account of the art and architecture of ancient Central America. Together with Coe 1993, these two books are essential to understanding the early history of Central America.

Tedlock, D. (tr.), *Popol Vuh: The Definitive Edition of the Mayan Book of the Dawn of Life and the Glories of Gods and Kings*, New York, 1985. Translation of the Mayan testament on the creation of the world.

Background to Guatemala, the country

De Koose, B.B., *Guatemala for You*, Guatemala, 1989. Concise and comprehensive guide to Guatemala.

Eltringham, P., J. Fisher & I. Stewart, *The Maya World: Rough Guide*, London, 1999. Up-to-date guide book with sensitivity to the history, politics and costumes of the country.

Kelsey, V. and L. de J. Osborne, *Four Keys to Guatemala*, New York, 1948. Comprehensive book on Guatemala, including a detailed list of 200 villages.

Menchú, R., *I, Rigoberta Menchú*, London, 1984. Moving account of the life of the Nobel Peace Prize winner: the realities of social and political struggle.

Costume/textiles

Altman, P.B. and C.C. West, *Threads of Identity: Maya Costume of the 1960s in Highland Guatemala*, Fowler Museum of Cultural History, University of California, 1992. Based on the museum's collection, with costumes grouped and compared according to their stylistic traits.

Anawalt, P.R., *Indian Clothing before Cortés: Mesoamerican Costumes from the Codices*, Norman, Oklahoma, 1981.

Anderson, M., *Guatemalan Textiles Today*, New York, 1978. During several visits to Guatemala the author learned to weave using the back-strap loom and interviewed and photographed the weavers. The result is a book full of technical information, amply illustrated by (mainly black-and-white) photographs.

Atwater, M.M., *Byways in Hand-weaving*, New York, 1954 (republished 1988). Includes weaving drafts for four Guatemalan belts.

Bertrand, R. and D. Magne, *The Textiles of Guatemala*, London, 1991. Published in Association with Liberty's of London to accompany Magne's exhibition, it is profusely illustrated with Bertrand's colour photographs.

Burnham, D.K., *A Textile Terminology: Warp & Weft*, London, 1981. A useful illustrated dictionary of weaving terms.

Deuss, K., *Indian Costumes from Guatemala*, London, 1981. Introduction to the textiles of Guatemala based on the author's own collection. Since publication, she has opened 'Maya: the Guatemala Indian Centre' in London.

Hecht, A., *The Art of the Loom: Weaving, Spinning and Dyeing across the World*, London, 1989. Eight chapters cover textiles from different parts of the world, including Guatemala.

Hecht, A., *Guatemalan Textiles*, to be published Spring 2001. A resumé of textiles from the Guatemalan Highlands in the British Museum, published as Occasional Paper no. 134

Neutze de Rugg, C., *Diseños en los Tejidos Indígenas de Guatemala*, Guatemala, 1986. The significance and meaning of designs throughout the country are described. Coloured plates illustrate designs set out on graph paper and embroidered.

Norton, C., *Tapestry Crochet: Dos Tejedoras*, Minnesota, 1991. Descriptions and diagrams of the type of crochet used by the Guatemalans to make bags.

O'Neale, L.M., *Textiles of Highland Guatemala*, Carnegie Institute, Washington, 1945. Classic text with numerous illustrations, covering every aspect of these textiles and the techniques used in their production.

Osborne, L. de J., *Indian Crafts of Guatemala and El Salvador*, University of Oklahoma Press, 1965. Readable account, well illustrated, of the Indians and their crafts, with textiles accounting for the whole of part 1.

Osborne, L. de J. and J. Wood, *Indian Costumes of Guatemala*, Austria, 1966. Osborne and Wood's text is complemented by line drawings of design motifs and sixty colour illustrations by Wood.

Pettersen, C.L., *Maya of/de Guatemala*, Guatemala, 1976. Large bilingual volume describing Guatemalan life and dress, with a full-page watercolour and facing description devoted to each of sixty towns and villages. Pettersen was born in Guatemala and studied art in London. After returning to the country of her birth she spent the rest of her life there, focusing on the Indians and their daily life.

Rowe, A.P., *A Century of Change*, Center for Inter-American Relations, New York, 1981. An expert on textiles, Rowe selects eleven towns and villages for an in-depth discussion of the changes taking place in their costume during the twentieth century.

Schevill, M.B., *Maya Textiles of Guatemala: The Gustavus A. Eisen Collection, 1902*, University of California, Berkeley, 1993. The Eisen Collection is the oldest in the United States and as such acts as a benchmark for studying the changes that occurred during the twentieth century.

Schevill, M.B., J.C. Berlo and E.B. Dwyer (eds), *Textile Traditions of Mesoamerica and the Andes*, University of Texas Press, 1996. The editors have brought together anthropologists, art historians and textile experts in one volume, within which there are many chapters relating to the textiles of Guatemala.

Schevill, M.B. (ed., with L. Asturias de Barrios), *The Maya Textile Tradition*, New York, 1997. This lavish volume, illustrated with superb photographs, takes an in-depth look at the life and art of the Maya of southern Mexico and Central America.

Sperlich, N. and E.K. Sperlich, *Guatemalan Backstrap Weaving*, University of Oklahoma Press, 1980. Detailed how-to-do-it instructions using photographs and line drawings.

Start, L.E., *The McDougall Collection of Indian Textiles from Guatemala and Mexico*, Oxford University Press, 1963. Detailed descriptions and line drawings of textiles in the Pitt Rivers Museum, Oxford.

museum accession numbers

PAGE	ACC. NO.						
2	1984 AM11.7		1973 AM 3.91 (RIGHT)	28	1980 Am 27.356	56	1980 Am 7.122
4	1984 AM11.1		1983 AM 13.2 (BELOW)	30	1980 Am 7.195	60	1973 Am 3.78
7	1973 AM 3.59 (TOP)	11	1980 AM 7.66	32	1980 Am 27.385	63	1973 Am 3.121
	1980 AM 27.129 (LEFT)	12	1980 AM 7.62A	35	1973 Am 3.19 & 20	64	1990 Am 13.1
		17	1980 AM 27.1&2	36	1983 Am 13.1	67	1983 Am 13.2
		18	1990 AM 13.3	39	1980 Am 27.383	69	1982 Am 16.7
		19	1980 AM 27.388	40	1980 Am 27.388	70	1980 Am 27.408
		22	1980 Am 27.4	43	1977 Am 5.10	74	1980 Am 27.401
		25	1984 Am 18.10	45	1980 Am 27.370	77	1973 Am 3.91
		26	1980 Am 27.129	49	1971 Am 23.11	78	1980 Am 27.415
				53	1971 Am 23.15	81	1980 Am 34.2
				55	1980 Am 7.169	INSIDE COVER	1984 AM 11. 9

publisher's acknowledgements

The textiles featured in this book are drawn from the collections of the British Museum's Department of Ethnography and have been selected from the viewpoint of their design and technical merit.

We should like to express our thanks to the many people who have helped us in the production of this book, and in particular from the Museum staff: Helen Wolfe, Elaine Dean and Mike Row. Paul Welti, the art director, must be credited not only for his arresting juxtaposition of illustrations and text, but also for his contribution to the captions analyzing the designs.

picture credits

index

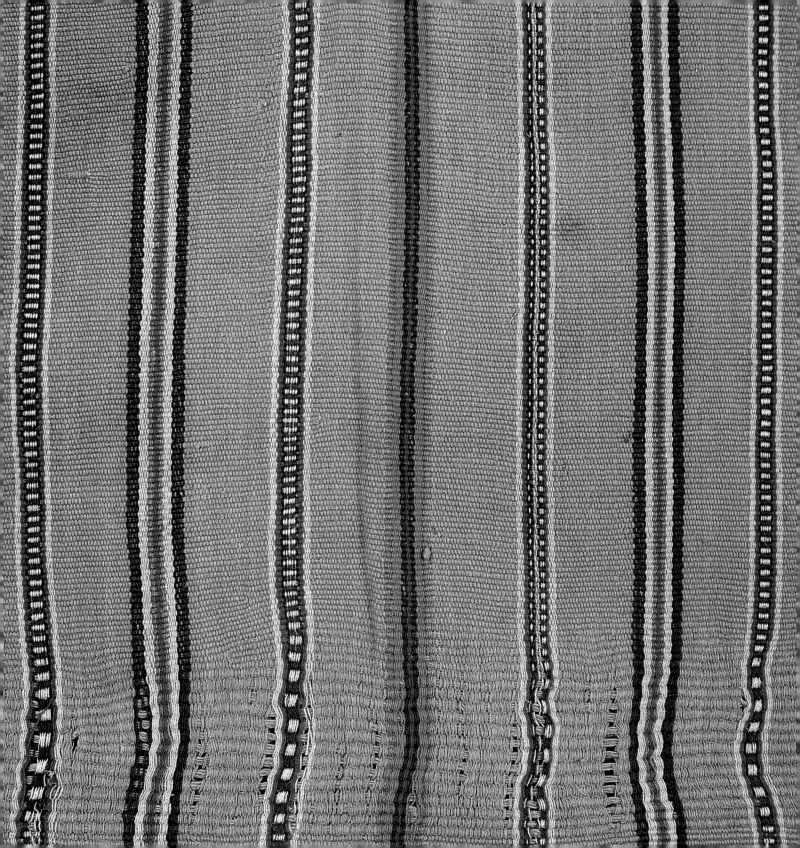